PAW PRINTS ON THE CAR

Viola K. Hunt

Illustrated by Grace E. Johnson

MINERVA PRESS

ATLANTA LONDON SYDNEY

PAW PRINTS ON THE CAR
Copyright © Viola K. Hunt 1999

All Rights Reserved

ISBN 0 75410 727 2

First Published 1999 by
MINERVA PRESS
315–317 Regent Street
London W1R 7YB

Printed in Great Britain for Minerva Press

PAW PRINTS ON THE CAR

FOREWORD

These poems are written for those who love cats, as well as for myself. The writing of these brought back many loving memories of the cats and kittens I have known. I can even remember certain events by recalling which cat ruled our house at that particular time.

Besides the incumbent(s) were the innumerable cats and kittens who found their way to our door, to stay until a good home could be found for them.

The noted author, Paul Gallico, wrote a book titled *The Honorable Cat* and this book led me to write these poems, or word pictures, of these wonderful animals as I have observed them at play or in deep thought.

I hope the reading is as enjoyable as was the writing.

Viola K. Hunt

APARTMENT CAT

Open the door
And let me out.
I was not meant to be
A prisoner in
Four rooms w/view.
When I was young
My needs were few;
Food,
Milk,
Shelter,
Love.
It was enough.
But I am older now and
The warm spring night sounds
Entreat me,

Call me,
Stirring my blood.
My body trembles with
Anguished yearning as
I claw the door
Moaning,
'Let me go.
Let me go.'

BLUE MONDAY

The cat next door
Challenged me.
I lost.
I broke the fishbowl
(I was only looking)
And was shown the door
Even though it was
Raining!
A dog chased me
Up a tree
And I couldn't remember
How to get down,
Temporarily.

Then
I pinched my nose
In the cupboard door.
I caught a mouse
But
It got away.
I should have believed
My horoscope for
Today.

FAIR WARNING

Dear lady,
Forgive me if
I do not share
Your delight
When tiny children
Come to call.
You, to whom I owe
My daily bowl of tuna,
Must accept the fact that
I do not like to be
Slapped,
Pulled,
Twitched,
Pinched,

Or sat upon.
I am not a dog;
Patient,
Long-suffering.
I am he who has
Claws
That scratch.
Consider all this
And understand.

HAVE A GOOD TRIP

It's all right if you leave me
Now and then.
Just make sure the sitter knows
The facts.
My catnip mouse…
Don't wash it,
It's fine just the way it is.
Keep my water dish full and
Take note of my favourite tuna.

Show her the chair that is
Mine alone.
Explain the subtle nuances
Of my cries.

One of your silken night-gowns
For my bed
Would be a nice thought
To keep me from forgetting you.

I believe that's all.
Have a good trip and
Try not to miss me
Too much.

CLEANLINESS IS NEXT TO…

Just as I had
Passed my tongue
Over every inch of me –
Stroked,
Brushed,
Rubbed,
Scoured,
Cleaned,
Burnished
And polished to an even sleekness –
You touched me,
And now it's to do
All over
Again!

COLOUR ME MISERY

Frightened,
Cold,
Hungry.
I run to meet
Each passer-by
And retreat
In despair.
I didn't know it was so easy
To get lost
While exploring
The world, but then,
I still have a lot
To learn.

CONTENTMENT

Rain
Outside.
Me
Inside,
Snug
On your lap,
Purring you
A song
Of
Love.

EXCUSEZ-MOI

I am young
And innocent.
How am I to know
that curtains
Are not meant
To be climbed?

FALLEN IDOL

Before the pyramids,
I was.
More powerful than
The Pharaohs
Was I.
A feline Deity.

Now I slink
Through the night
In the rain.
Homeless,
Hungry.
Revered no more.

FELINE REFLECTIONS

Being a kitten
Is easy.
Becoming a cat
Takes time.
Be patient.

FORBIDDEN DELIGHTS

Ahh!
This is
The way
To spend
The day;
Basking in the sun
On the table.
Of course I know I shouldn't
But then,
No one is home.

GREETINGS, STRANGER

I turn my back on you.
Don't expect me
To show delight
At your return.
You left me
In a strange place
With strangers!
I felt forsaken
How was I to know
You would return?

No. No.
Your blandishments
Are wasted on me.

It's possible that
I might forgive you
Later.
But not yet.

I THINK THAT I SHALL NEVER SEE... ETC.

Blame it on my youth,
If blame you must place,
And get me down
From this swaying,
Bending
Tree-top.
No lectures, please.
I'm not listening
Anyway.
My pitiful cries
Should make it plain to see

That the next move
Is not up to
Me.

MAYBE I NEED A PSYCHIATRIST

If I look worried,
It's because I am.
I worry a lot;
If I climb that tree
And I can't get down,
Who will rescue me?
Suppose I eat all my food
And then
Nobody fills the dish again?

I worry about this too;
What if you go out that door
And don't come back?

Kittens need security
And only you
Can give me that.

THANKSGIVING

I hate
Loud voices,
Pointing fingers,
And threatening gestures.
It offends my
Dignity.
Therefore,
I am leaving
(If you will open the door).
What if I did sample
The turkey?

I thought I was one of
the family.
Apparently
I was wrong.

I Am Cat

I cannot be owned
Nor possessed.
Give me respect
And freedom to roam,
And chances are
I'll never leave home.

I SHOULD HAVE HAD IT GIFT-WRAPPED

Head erect,
Eyes aglow
With the joy of giving,
I dropped my gift
Into your lap;
A mouse –
A most delectable mouse.
Then fled in terror
As your screams
Echoed through the
House.

IT's ALL IN THE MOTION

You know
I get sick
When
I ride
In a car.
And I did.
Very.

KITTEN IN A TREE-TOP

Don't bother to
Plead,
Coax,
Cajole
Or threaten me.
I'm not listening
Anyway.
I *know* how I got up.
The trick,
I find,
Is getting down.

LISTEN, DOG

Stay right where you are.
Don't think that because
I am small,
You can win this fight.
No sir,
Size means nothing.
Observe my ridged back
And unsheathed claws.
I know I am
A fearsome sight.
So pause, consider, and then
Run!

LOVE STORY

When
Your fingers smooth
My fur
And scratch
My eager chin
As you whisper endearments
In my ear,
My body trembles
And I fear that
I shall die
Of love.

MERRY CHRISTMAS

I thought
You brought
This tree
For me
To climb.
Apparently
I was wrong.
Now I sit
Amidst the ruins –
I didn't know
I was so
Strong.

MIRROR MIRROR

Stranger,
Come out from behind
That wall,
So we can meet.
It's plain to see
That you are just
Like me
In your movements
And grace.
Let's be friends.
I'm willing
If you are.

NOBODY'S PERFECT

Kittens do come in many colours;
Orange and white,
Black and white,
Or maybe all three combined.
Does it really matter?
It only proves that even a Blue Ribbon cat,
An aristocratic feline,
Is prone to
An occasional weakness
(As you can plainly see)
If given the opportunity.

OPHELIA

Are they not beautiful –
My babies?
And I did it all
By myself.
Well…
Almost.
The father?
Who knows?
I was drunk
With
The moon
That night.

PAW PRINTS ON THE CAR

'Tis much ado about nothing,
At least from my point of view.
It's not as if I have damaged your car,
It's only a paw print or two.

PLAY WITH ME

Feint and dodge,
Dart to and fro,
Hide and seek
Beneath the sheet.
I lie very still
So you won't find me
Although I know you will.
Making beds is fun.

SERENDIPITY

A fence is for
Sitting on,
While
Serenely contemplating
The dog
On the other side;
Frustrated,
Enraged,
Dancing a
Frenzied
Two-step.

Doesn't he know
That I am
Invincible?

THE EXPLORER

What is in
This box,
That bag,
That open drawer?
Oh!
So much to see,
So much to explore.

THE PUGILIST

Spare me your
Tongue cluckings
And 'tut tuts'.
Just wash off the blood,
Feed me,
And let me rest.
There's another full moon
Tonight.

YOU'LL WALK ALONE

A leash
On me?
Ridiculous.
Try it
And you'll see
That Houdini had
Nothing
On me.